Little Book of
GUIDANCE

INNERLIGHT
PUBLISHING

Welcome to our Inner Light
Little book of GUIDANCE

This book comes with the intention to help the user to take a deep breath, relax and
reflect on the word for the day to bring about a state of peace and serenity.
When you take a few minutes here and there throughout your day to check in with yourself and your state. It will help to expand your awareness of what is happening within you, which then can empower you to change your thoughts from something negative to something positive. Focusing on a positive thought or word will not only brighten up your inner state but it can also brighten up the state of others around you.
Inner Light wishes you many wonderful light hearted and peaceful days.

How to use this book

Step 1. Take a few deep breathes focusing on each breath.

Step2. Ask to be guided to what you most need in this moment.

Step3. Randomly open the book and look at the word on the page.

Step4. Contemplate the word throughout your day. Write down whatever comes to you, and share the word around with family and friends.

Step5. At the end of the day take note of the positive effects the word had on you and others and thank your guides for bringing the word to you.

Use the book daily to maintain a positive approach to life.

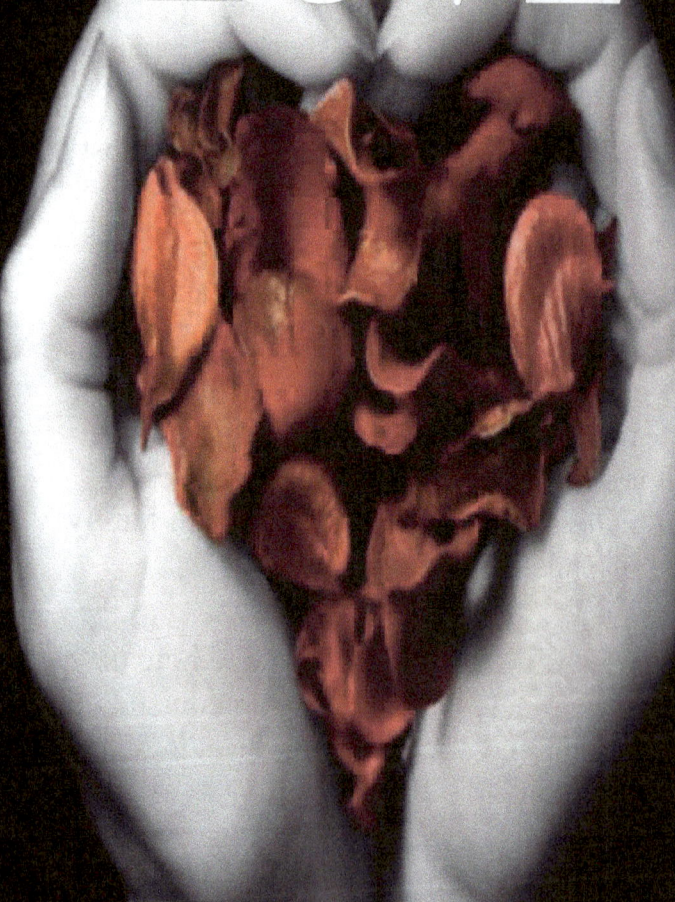

HAPPINESS

Feeling happy attracts more things to be happy about

Karen Mc Dermott

TRUST

Trust in the process of life and you will reach new heights

Karen Mc Dermott

FAITH

Faith unites all things with a higher power
Lucy Pignataro

SHARING

Sharing opens the heart and soul
Lucy Pignataro

BALANCE

When we find balance we find harmony

Karen Mc Dermott

RESTORE

Restore your spirit back to it's original oneness with divinity

Lucy Pignataro

NURTURE

Never underestimate the power of nurturing

Lucy Pignataro

BLESSINGS

Count your blessings, you already have more than you think

Lucy Pignataro

KINDNESS

Kindness is one of the greatest gifts you can give to another.

Lucy Pignataro

GENTLENESS

Gentleness feels as soft as a new born baby

Lucy Pignataro

SELF CARE

Nurture your mind, body and soul just because you're worth it

Lucy Pignataro

COURAGE

It only takes a small spark to ignite the courage within

Lucy Pignataro

GRATITUDE

Expressing gratitude enriches all humanity.
Lucy Pignataro

SHINE

When you allow your light to shine brightly you enable others to do the same.

Lucy Pignataro

EXERCISE

A good dose of exercise lightens the load

Lucy Pignataro

MINDFULNESS

Being mindful means living life
consciously and with meaning

Lucy Pignataro

SILENCE

Peace is restored when you make a choice to sit in silence and listen to the voice of your spirit

Lucy Pignataro

TOLERANCE

A little bit of tolerance goes along way

Lucy Pignataro

PRAYER

The power of pray will transform your life like nothing else

Lucy Pignataro

SELF-LOVE

Only when we love ourselves
will we know true love.

Lucy Pignataro

FEARLESSNESS

You will never know how strong you are until you are standing on the edge of destruction

Lucy Rignataro

SELF RESPECT

When we have self respect we have the respect of others

Lucy Pignataro

BREATHE

Take a slow deep breath in
and a long easeful breath out,
it will work wonders

Lucy Pignataro

PATIENCE

All things can be accomplished
with
a little bit of patience
Lucy Pignataro

STAMINA

Stamina will take you all the way to achieving your dreams.
Lucy Pignataro

S
M
I
L
E

When we smile our heart shines and the world smiles with us

Lucy Pignataro

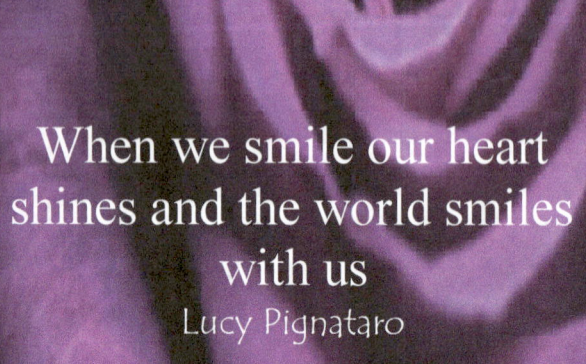

HUGS

Hug your family, hug a friend, hug a stranger, hug a tree just share a hug there is nothing better

Lucy Pignataro

DANCE

Unleash your inner god/goddess and dance like nobody's watching

Lucy Pignataro

YOGA

Yoga is meditation in motion,
a great way to relax
Lucy Pignataro

Use this space to jot down words that resonate with you

About Lucy Pignataro

Lucy Pignataro is and always has been both inquisitive and passionate about life and the way we live it.

Continually aspiring to look for the best in herself and ours. As a Counselor, Life coach and Reiki therapist that Lucy helps others to find their way and aspire to better ways of living. As a wife and mother she finds joy and fulfillment in sharing her life with the people she loves unconditionally and that are a great source of encouragement and inspiration.

It is Lucy intention that through this sharing of her life experiences and lessons that others are encouraged to bring forth their gifts and wisdom.

You can purchase Lucy's other books *In Search of my Soul*, her *Life Journal*, *Dream Journal* and *Prayer Diary* at your preferred online retailer or by visiting www.innerlightpublish.com

About Karen Mc Dermott

Karen Mc Dermott began her writing journey at adoptamum.com. in 2010. Filled to the brim with creativeness after having her 4th child she began writing short pieces of interest, this soon grew into featured articles and then her first novel *The Visitor* was born through the belief and support she received from adoptamum.com. Consistently building upon her desire to write, learn and help others she has now published her second novel *The Wish Giver* and her third, *The Memory Taker* is due for release in 2013.

You can purchase Karen's books *The Visitor*, *The Wish Giver* and her journals *Gratitude Diary*, *Inspiration Journal* and *Attraction Journal* at your preferred online retailer or by visiting www.innerlightpublish.com

Produced by Inner Light Publishing
Printed by Lightning source ltd, Melbourne, Australia

The author retains copyright.

ISBN : **978-0-9922820-0-4**
eBook **978-0-9922820-1-1**

www.ingramcontent.com/pod-product-compliance
Lightning Source LLC
Chambersburg PA
CBHW072115290426
44110CB00014B/1919